A Wilderness Habitat Discovery Book

the Rocky Mountains

written & illustrated
by
Robert Bullock

HOMESTEAD PUBLISHING
Moose, Wyoming

DEDICATED

To Sarah Irvin Bullock
whose gift of teaching has touched many, many lives.

Published by
HOMESTEAD PUBLISHING
Box 193
Moose, Wyoming 83014

INTRODUCTION

This book is one of a series of **Wilderness Habitats** for young readers written to help stimulate their curiosity and interest in our environment. Children and parents learn about the natural flora and fauna of America's great habitats through the experiences of well-known historical naturalists.

CLUE-Q is intended to encourage readers of all ages to discover the secrets of nature. In the story are clues to help solve the answer to each fascinating natural subject. The answers to **Clue-Q** are provided in the back of the book. Adults are encouraged to read the story with their children and to look for clues.

Jedediah Smith glanced up to see angular peaks in the high country of the Rocky Mountains. He had ridden for days through the tall grass of the Great Plains, and in the far distance had seen the snow-covered peaks erupting upwards from the flat landscape.

The easiest trail for Jedediah ran along a chain of lakes at the foot of the mountains. The tougher trails climbed through canyons formed by glaciers a long time ago. Jedediah was lonelier when he took those tougher trails. But, at the base of the mountains Jedediah welcomed the shade from the **ponderosa pine** forest.

During the day it can get as hot on these lower mountain slopes as it does on the Plains. It gets much cooler at night because the dry mountain air cannot hold the heat.

The pack string jogged along behind Jedediah as he headed for a campsite at a higher elevation.

The **Rocky Mountains** are located in the western United States. The mountains form a chain that extends from Canada, where they are known as the Canadian Rockies, south through the United States.

A scream like that of a hawk prompted Jedediah to turn quickly in his saddle. Looking up, he saw a **steller's jay** perched on the limb of a ponderosa pine tree. It is a common blue, crested jay of the mountain forests, and it can mimic the scream of a hawk.

Several **monarch butterflies** skipped on the hot breezes around patches of blue lupine flowers. Finally, they landed on a tree branch. To Jedediah, these butterflies were a weather sign because they winter in Mexico, then migrate north for the summer.

CLUE–Q *What season of the year is it?*

Continuing on the trail, Jedediah noticed several trees with their upper bark torn off. The shredded "bear trees" had marks higher than those made by black bears, and a yellowish brown tuft of hair was left hanging.

Jedediah felt a shiver; his eyes scanned the terrain.

Water cascaded from a high cleft.

Appearing from behind a stand of juniper trees a **grizzly bear** paused and her white-tipped hairs glittered. Jedediah positioned his team slowly and carefully downwind so the bear could not sense their presence. She loped over to the nearby stream followed by two bear cubs. Though their diet is primarily vegetarian—roots, leaves, nuts, berries—they also enjoy eating small mammals and fish.

CLUE–Q *What were the bears seeking in the stream?*

While the cubs waited, the mother bear waded into the shallow part of the stream. Moving carefully, she scooped a **cutthroat trout** from the water with her giant claws. Its reddish jaw glistened in the twilight. The fish flipped about the grass as the cubs pounced on it. After they had eaten enough they wandered off.

To Jedediah's surprise a **beaver** waddled to the water's edge after the bears had left the area. Its tail was flat and hairless. Beavers cut down willow and aspen saplings for food. This beaver slid into the water and paddled upstream to its lodge near the dam.

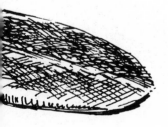

By now Jedediah had decided an early start in the morning would get him through the pass. He set up his camp and bedded his horses.

The peaceful night was disturbed only by the deep resonant hooting of the **great horned owl**. The largest and best known of the common owls, they are believed to possess supernatural powers because they see in the dark.

24

As the sky began to lighten a sharp loud "peek" of a **hairy woodpecker** resounded. Jedediah was curious and followed the sounds. The male woodpecker drummed faster as Jedediah neared. It had a white back and black wings with white spots and a bright red patch showed below the crown of the head.

CLUE–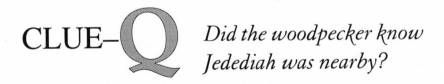 *Did the woodpecker know Jedediah was nearby?*

The pine trees around the woodpecker were tall with a narrow, dense conical crown. These were **lodgepole pine** trees whose slender trunks or poles were used by Native Americans to support their tents or teepees.

CLUE–Q   *How did the lodgepole get its name?*

While walking back to his campsite, Jedediah saw several **mountain bluebirds** circling low in the sky. They dropped fast trying to catch insects floating in the winds. He could also hear their quiet warbling song echoing through the forest.

Camouflaged in the brown and green grass of the pasture a **snowshoe hare** waited cautiously. Also called the varying hare, the snowshoe gets its name because its color varies with the seasons.

CLUE– *What color was the hare presently?*

Opposite the campsite a bull **American elk** appeared with a fine set of antlers on his head. He stood proud and tall ready for rutting, a mating battle. Jedediah noticed tree seedlings stripped of their growth.

CLUE– *Was the elk male or female?*

As Jedediah was packing, he glanced up to see the graceful descent of a **bald eagle,** the best known of eagles in North America. The rising sun highlighted its snow-white head and tail.

The eagle swooped down to the pasture and caught the hare in its talons. The eagle then flew off to its tree top home.

Jedediah and his pack horses skirted a forest opening containing clusters of **Indian paintbrush** flowers. The roots of the paintbrush act like a parasite by connecting to roots of other plants to get water.

Jedediah's horse shuffled small pebbles that littered the trail. The small rocks dislodged a brown **meadow vole** from its hiding place.

This creature, the most common of mountain mammals, can create interconnecting burrows under snow where it hides from predators.

But now the vole was exposed to danger.

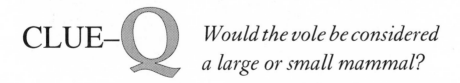

CLUE–Q *Would the vole be considered a large or small mammal?*

Not far away a **wandering garter snake** had retreated into a grassy patch. The dull gray snake peered out with its head held high— waiting for Jedediah to pass before it attacked the vole.

CLUE– *Why was the wandering garter snake afraid?*

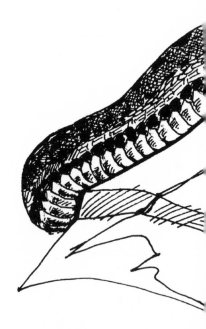

The slope became steeper.

The thinning forest was left behind as Jedediah rode above the timberline.

He rode carefully weaving along the rocky path, bypassing many delicate **subalpine buttercups**. Their brilliant yellow petals were open to the penetrating sunshine. Only occasionally did he encounter a steep drop of the mountain side.

43

As he moved past a rocky ledge, Jedediah noticed some plants—grasses and sedges and thistles—laid out on the rocks. This was a curious practice of the **pika**, a small brownish rodent. It was drying out its food for the coming winter.

Jedediah Smith's horse stopped short and shifted uneasily.

A **mountain lion** leaped to a perch on the rocks very close by.

Was it after another animal? Was it trailing Jedediah? Though curious about human beings, mountain lions do not ordinarily attack them.

CLUE–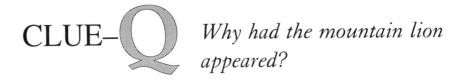 *Why had the mountain lion appeared?*

Poised on a ledge above Jedediah was a **bighorn sheep,** among the rarest of wild animals in North America. Its massive brown horns curled up and back over the ears in a C-shape.

The lion eyed the ram, and, perhaps, daydreamed of catching him. Jedediah waited for the drama to unfold.

The lion waited patiently.

The ram eased down the near vertical cliffside. His hooves are hard at the outer edge and soft at the center to provide traction on the rocks.

The lion leaped after the ram, but the ram, being cautious, sprinted off among the rocks.

The wind blowing through the pass was a welcom
relief to the heat of the day. Jedediah edged his horse forwar
along the mountain trail. Then he began his descent.

A yellow-bellied marmot scurried away to its home in the rock crevices where it chirped and whistled until Jedediah had passed.

The subalpine meadow into which Jedediah rode
was carpeted with flowers of the **avalanche lily**. This
mountain wildflower blooms after the snow melts, and is
attached to a stalk with two broad leaves at the base.

The area was bright from the reflected sunlight off the
snowy white petals.

Jedediah was a trapper, and on this journey he had not been lonely. All the creatures he had seen were adapted to the mixed climate of the Rocky Mountains.

As he rode slowly back onto the forested slopes, Jedediah thought of the pioneers on the Plains coming West. The pass was one of the few places to cross the great Rocky Mountain chain.

Jedediah was tired, and his cabin home was not far away now.

CLUE AND ANSWERS

Page 13   *What season of the year is it?*
                  Clues: hot; north for the summer
                  Answer: summer

Page 14   *What were the bears seeking in the stream?*
                  Clues: fish
                  Answer: food

Page 25   *Did the woodpecker know Jedediah was nearby?*
                  Clues: woodpecker drummed faster
                  Answer: yes

Page 27   *How did the lodgepole get its name?*
                  Clues: used by the Indians for lodges
                  Answer: product of the Indian culture

Page 30   *What color was the hare presently?*
                  Clues: color varies with the seasons; camouflaged
                  Answer: brown

Page 32   *Was the elk male or female?*
Clues: bull; he; his
Answer: male

Page 39   *Would the vole be considered a large or small*
mammal?
Clues: small rocks
Answer: small

Page 40   *Why was the wandering garter snake afraid?*
Clues: retreated; waited for Jedediah to pass
Answer: Jedediah

Page 46   *Why had the mountain lion appeared?*
Clues: do not ordinarily attack human beings
Answer: after another animal

NEW WORDS

adapted (v) to modify, change or adjust to a new situation or
    condition

crown (n) the top of the head

descent (v) the action of going, or coming down

diet (n) different types of food which are eaten

erupting (v) to burst forth

migrate (v) to go from one place to another

mimic (v) to resemble, to be like or copy

parasite (n) an animal or plant which lives in or upon another

shallow (adj) not deep; not far from the surface

supernatural (adj) unnaturally extraordinary

timberline (n) an area on the mountain side, above which
    trees do not grow

warbling (v) a vibrating or quivering of sound

INDEX

ABOUT THE AUTHOR

Mr. Bullock is presently the Chief of Exhibition Management at the State Museum of Pennsylvania.

He first thought of the Wilderness Habitat series while working for the American Museum of Natural History in New York City, and his first book, *The Great Plains*, was published while working as a museum exhibit designer at Yale University's Peabody Museum of Natural History.

Mr. Bullock writes and illustrates books for children and designs interactive museum exhibits. He is in 1991 *Who's Who in the East.*